HE ... APERS

Early Medieval Archaeology in Western Europe – Its History and Development

by

Richard Hodges

HEADSTART HISTORY

Published by HEADSTART HISTORY
PO Box 41, Bangor, Gwynedd LL57 1SB

Set by MEDCALF TYPE LTD
Launton, Bicester, Oxon

Printed by THE IPSWICH BOOK COMPANY LTD
The Drift, Nacton Road
Ipswich, Suffolk IP3 3QR

ISBN 1 873041 11 X
A CIP catalogue record for this book is available from the British Library

TO
PETER ADDYMAN

who introduced me to the European dimension of Early Medieval Archaeology

ACKNOWLEDGEMENTS

I am a always conscious of the debt that I owe to my friends, who have taken the time to debate the issues described here. In particular, my thanks to Anders Andrén, Martin Carver, Gian-Pietro Brogiolo, Paolo Delogu, Riccardo Francovich, Federico Marazzi, John Moreland, John Mitchell, Klavs Randsborg, Frans Theuws, and Chris Wickham for sharing their ideas with me.

Richard Hodges
British School at Rome

CONTENTS

Frontispiece: A reconstruction drawing of Hamwic, Anglo-Saxon Southampton as it was c. 700. Note the boundary ditch on the left-hand side and the wide main street. (Courtesy of Southampton City Museums.)

INTRODUCTION

The HEADSTART HISTORY PAPERS aim to identify important themes and topics the significance of which extends beyond the studies of professional historians. The PAPERS are distillations of the research of distinguished scholars in a form appropriate to sixth formers, undergraduates and the general reader.

The essay was originally written in Italian and was commissioned by Paolo Delogu and Riccardo Francovich for a supplement of the popular Italian archaeology magazine *Archeo*. The brief was to provide an accessible overview of how archaeology was shedding new light on a number of familiar historical debates about the early middle ages. The result, not unexpectedly, is a synthesis of Dr. Hodges' research on this subject in northern Europe and Italy. The substance of this research affirms the need for a closer collaboration between archaeologists and historians in active research projects. It aims to illustrate the achievements of archaeologists of the early medieval period, whose efforts begin to offer the means to shape a new history of the first millennium.

Richard Hodges studied archaeology and medieval history at Southampton University, where he wrote a doctorate on the imported Carolingian pottery from Hamwic, Anglo-Saxon Southampton. He joined Sheffield University in 1976 as a lecturer in the Department of Archaeology & Prehistory. He has been a visiting professor at SUNY-Binghamton, Copenhagen and Siena Universities. He has excavated in Britain, Italy and Turkey; his principal archaeological fieldwork has been the landscape archaeology of Roystone Grange, the deserted medieval village of Montarrenti, Tuscany and the early Benedictine abbey of San Vincenzo al Volturno. His books include *The Hamwih Pottery* (1981), *Dark Age Economics* (1982), (with David Whitehouse), *Mohammed, Charlemagne & the Origins of Europe* (1983), (with John Mitchell), *San Vincenzo al Volturno* (1985), *Primitive and Peasant Markets* (1988), *The Anglo-Saxon Achievement* (1989) and *Wall-to-Wall History* (1991).

Every author in this series has made a distinguished contribution to their subject. Richard Hodges is currently Director of The British School at Rome and I am delighted and honoured that he agreed to present a paper.

JUDITH LOADES
Bangor, 1991

I

HISTORIOGRAPHY

The origins of Medieval Archaeology are rooted in the recent development of History. Antiquarians carried out excavations of medieval sites as long ago as the Renaissance, but they believed that little connection existed between the material culture and the history they uncovered. Even nineteenth-century antiquarians like Thomas Bateman in England or Hjalmar Stolpe in Sweden had a limited grasp of the historical significance of their archaeological discoveries. During the 1840's, for example, Bateman opened dozens of Anglo-Saxon graves, and described their contents fully in his two books *Vestiges of the Antiquities or Derbyshire* (1848) and *Ten Years Digging in Celtic and Saxon Grave-hills* (1861). But he considered the people in the graves he rudely excavated to be simply expressions of a past charted by historians. First and foremost, Bateman and his friends were interested in the excitement of discovery – an excitement captured in a poem written about him:

> 'Uprouse ye, then, my barrow-digging men,
> It is our opening day!
> And all exclaimed, their grog whilst swigging,
> There's naught on earth like barrow digging!'

---

1 Stephen Isaacson, *Barrow-Digging by a Barrow-Knight,* (London 1845). See also Barry Marsden, *The Barrow Knight* (A biography of Thomas Bateman), (Shipley 1988).

Hjalmar Stolpe (1841-1905) represents a considerable advance on this antiquarianism. In many ways he was a great technician, concerned to collect and record the data as fully as possible. His most distinguished excavation was the great Viking cemetery at Birka in the Mälar region of central Sweden. Here, between 1873 and 1895, he painstakingly excavated 1100 graves recording the soils and the contents of each one in uparalleled detail. Finally, each grave was drawn to scale on graph paper. Stolpe's field drawings are so good that most have been published during the course of the 20th century[2]. In the history of archaeology, Stolpe has been forgotten. Instead, Heinrich Schliemann's excavations at Mycenae and Troy, Arthur Evans' excavations at Knossos, and the excavations of Rodolfo Lanciani and Giacomo Boni in the Forum of Rome – all undertaken at much the same time – have continued to capture far greater attention. Of course, this reflects the strong thread of classicism in Western society, which gained especially great influence during the 19th century[3]. The archaeology of the Vikings in the late 19th century, even if it was the richest cemetery beside the most important Viking settlement in Scandinavia, was not a matter of any special interest.

In charting the history of Medieval Archaeology Stolpe's excavations should not be forgotten. There is little doubt that the Viking antiquities that he uncovered were well-known to J. H. Holwerda when, just after the First World War, he carried out excavations of the trading town of Dorestad, near the mouth of the Rhine in the Netherlands. Holwerda's

---

2 See Anne-Sofie Gräslund, *Birka IV: The Burial Customs*, (Stockholm 1980).

3 See Richard Jenkyns, *The Victorians and Ancient Greece*, (London 1980); Frank Turner, *The Greek Heritage in Victorian Britain*, (London 1980); Richard Hodges, Glyn Daniel, the Great Divide, and the British Contribution to Italian archeology, *The Accordia Research Papers*, 1 (1990), 83-93.

excavations were also stimulated by the work of L. D. F. Janssen, a 19th-century antiquarian, who had collected material from its cemeteries and studied the history and topography of the lost settlement. Like Birka, Dorestad had been an international centre in the early Middle Ages, and its re-discovery undoubtedly fuelled the imagination of a number of archaeologists and historians at the time[4]. Perhaps the most influential of these has been the German archaeologist, Herbert Jankuhn who in 1930 began a campaign of excavations at Hedeby, the deserted, walled settlement near Schleswig in north Germany. Jankuhn began by putting a cutting through the huge earthen wall around the settlement. But in 1934 he opened a large area inside the walls, and carefully revealed the archaeology of part of the settlement. These excavations, the first of many campaigns that continue today, made an enormous impression upon archaeologists and historians at the time. Their real impact, however, has been obscured to some extent by the fact that Jankuhn became increasingly fascinated by the SS and their ideology[5].

As more than fifty years have passed since Jankuhn's book was published, it is possible to take a historical perspective of these circumstances. No-one can condone the Nazis, yet Jankuhn, in fact, belonged to a generation of German scholars who were fascinated by the early rise of Germany. In some ways they were also swept along by changes in the

---

4 On Dorestad see W. J. H. Verwers, Dorestad: a Carolingian town?, in R. Hodges & B. Hobley (eds.), *The Rebirth of the town in the West, AD 700-1050,* (London 1988); for the old excavations: J. H. Holwerda, Opgravingen van Dorestad, *Oudheidkundige Mededeelingen,* 9 (1930), 32-96.

5 Herbert Jankuhn, *Haithabu: Ein Handelsplatz der Wikingerzeit,* (Neumünster 1937); Bettina Arnold, The past as propaganda in Nazi Germany, *Antiquity,* 64 (1990), 464-78 at 474.

conventions of historiography. Notions of inter-disciplinary research were being introduced by the young, so-called *Annales* historians of the Sorbonne at Paris[6]. Similarly, questions were being asked about social and economic history, which were difficult for traditional medievalists to answer without reference to the material culture. Herbert Jankuhn's generation had the opportunity to draw the curtain back from a great panorama of history that had lain concealed. Of course, many of the great German scholars of this period, were forced to flee the country after 1933. Yet the extraordinary work of art historians and archaeologists like Ernst Kitzinger, Richard Krautheimer, Erwin Panofsky and Joachim Werner bears witness to an unabashed interest in reconstructing a romantic, over-arching history of Europe in which, not unexpectedly, Germany figures prominently.

Perhaps the most imaginative expression of the acadamic spirit of the 'thirties can be traced to the first major synthesis of Medieval Archaeology. Published in 1937, Holger Arbman's *Schweden und das karolingische Reich* remains a classic study of the Viking Age and its connections. Arbman's book arose out of his studies of the documentation of Birka left by Hjalmar Stolpe after he died. In many ways it has been overlooked as a prologue to his huge catalogues describing the graves from Birka, published during the 'forties[7]. Yet, it was an attempt to use archaeology in order to rewrite the history of the Baltic Sea communities during the Carolingian Age. This was a new type of history, very similar to Jankuhn's in some respect, although Arbman disapproved of what was

---

6 A readable introduction to the *annales* school may be found in Peter Burke, *The French Historical Revolution*, (Cambridge 1990).

7 E. H. Arbman, *Schwden und das karolingische Reich*, (Stockholm 1937); E. H. Arbman, *Birka I, Die Gräber*, Tafeln, (Stockholm 1940); Text, (Stockholm 1943).

taking place at Hedeby. Arbman's book, it might be said, marks the birth of Medieval Archeology as a scientific discipline.

Elswhere in Europe in the 'thirties the prospects for using archaeology to write history were not overlooked. The work of Arbman and Jankuhn, for example, was well-known in Britain, where R. E. M. Wheeler, the extraordinary director of the London Museum, encouraged a young archaeologist called G. C. Dunning to record the archaeology of building-sites in London. Wheeler then found a young Oxford graduate, John Ward-Perkins, to complete a catalogue of all the collections. In Wheeler's mind, this curated collection would provide the basis for scientific investigations in the future – a policy he adopted when he later became responsible for archaeology in India[8].

In Italy there was greater concern during the 'thirties with uncovering the age of Augustus. Nonetheless, it should be remembered that Richard Krautheimer began his great 5-volume study of the Early Christian and Early Medieval churches of Rome during this period, the *Corpus Basilicarum Christianarum Romae.* Similarly G. P. Bonetti was making analytical studies of the medieval topography and early Medieval Archaeology of Brescia, Castelseprio and Milan, which, in common with the strange spirit of the age, were European in their orientation[9].

---

8 Jacquetta Hawkes, *Mortimer Wheeler: Adventurer in Archaeology,* (London 1982); John Hurst, Gerald Dunning and his contribution to Medieval Archaeology, *Medieval Ceramics* 6 (1982), 3-20; John Ward-Perkins, *Museum Medieval Catalogue, no.* 7, (London 1940).

9 See Riccardo Francovich's introduction to his edited book: *Archeologia e Storia del Medievo Italiano,* (Rome 1987). Richard Krautheimer, *Corpus Basilicarum Christianorum Romae,* Vatican, Rome, 1 (1937); 2 (1959); 3 (1964); 4 (1970); 5 (1977)

Medieval Archaeology came of age swiftly after the Second World War. The renewal of bombed cities offered many city museums a hitherto unprecedented opportunity to investigate the early, undocumented beginnings of town life. Major excavations in this period took place in Cologne, Emden, Hamburg, London and Southampton. At Southampton, for example, excavations were initiated in the bombed docklands to look for the West Saxon port of *Hamwic,* mentioned in the written sources of the 8th and 9th centuries. The early interim reports describing these investigations tellingly reveal the influence of Jankuhn's research at Hedeby, and the ever-present prospect of discovering finds that might be paralleled with those from Birka[10]. Excavations in many German towns, notably Cologne and Hamburg, led to a rich reappraisal of urban history. Over the course of several decades, as a result, the early history of Cologne cathedral was reconstructed. While at Hamburg the early history of the fortified bishop's palace, destroyed by the Vikings, in some ways continued, if a litte less explicitly, the research initiated by Jankuhn.

Outside the towns, though, there was now also an interest in village history. The pioneers of this in Britain came from history departments; in 1947 M. W. Beresford, a lecturer in economic history at Leeds University and W. G. Hoskins, a lecturer in economics at Leicester University, began carrying out a number of small-scale excavations in deserted medieval villages to help them make sense of what was evidently a major feature of the Middle Ages. In many respects they wished to extend the experience of E. T. Leeds, a keeper of antiquities at the Ashmolean Museum, Oxford,

---

10 For a description of these early excavations see P. V. Addyman & D. H. Hill, Saxon Southampton: a review of the evidence, part I, *Proceedings of the Hampshire Field Club,* 24-25 (1968), 61-93.

who during the 'twenties had excavated (albeit rather crudely) a large part of an Anglo-Saxon village at Sutton Courtenay (Oxfordshire)[11]. Technically, the excavations of Beresford and Hoskins were no better than those of Leeds, and failed to make sense of the archaeology for the purpose they needed as a historians. Nevertheless, Beresford pursued the idea of digging sites, and in 1952 was trenching the well-preserved deserted medieval village of Wharram Percy in the Yorkshire Wolds when J. G. Hurst, recently graduated from Cambridge, encountered him. Hurst and his colleague Jack Golson (later Professor of Archaeology at Canberra University) persuaded Beresford to devise a project, which took shape as the Wharram Research Project, and to introduce the kind of open-area excavation techniques that the German refugee, Gerhard Bersu had used during the war to uncover a complex series of superimposed Viking structures at Vowlam on the Isle of Man. This was the beginning of the most influential project in British and, possibly, European Medieval Archaeology in recent times[12].

The Wharram Research Project focusses upon the changing morphology of the village and its environs (its fields etc.) over the past two millennia. Over the course of forty seasons it has demonstrated the changing shape of the settlement, its material culture, its habitat and its environs. This has had a great impact upon British social and economic history, providing a quantifiable measure of village life from Roman times until the present century.

---

11 J. G. Hurst, A Review of Archaeological Research, in M. W. Beresford & J. G. Hurst (eds.), *Deserted Medieval Village Studies*, (London 1971), 76-89; E. T. Leeds, A Saxon village near Sutton Courtenay, Berkshire, *Archaeologia* XXIII, (1923), 147-92.

12 M. W. Beresford & J. G. Hurst, *Wharram Percy*, (London 1990).

Hurst was also an important figure (with Sir David Wilson) in founding the Society for Medieval Archaeology in 1956, emulating the societies concerned with Prehistoric and Roman studies. In its early years, especially, the Society provided a forum for developing research strategies, as well as improving the collection of data as a basis for scientific investigation. Its membership, it might claim, enthusiastically pushed along the concept of rescue archaeology in towns and the countryside as urban renewal and rural development in the 'sixties entered a new phase. As a result, during the later 'sixties and 'seventies there were dozens of urban excavations as well as many landscape projects imitating the experience at Wharram Percy. Nowadays, there are more than fifty professional archaeological units employing several thousand people, whose largest interest is Medieval Archaeology. This recent history has been repeated elsewhere in Western Europe. Journals concerned with Medieval Archaeology were founded in France in 1971, Italy in 1974 and West Germany in 1975. In addition, there is a regular series of conferences entitled the Chateau Gaillard conference, founded in 1963, which are concerned with the archaeology of the castle in Western Europe. The British experience in rescue archaeology has also been widely imitated. For example, for a while British archaeologists formed the greater part of those excavating in Norwegian towns, and it was the Council for British Archaeology's strategy for urban archaeology which was adopted in Sweden by the antiquities' service. Similarly, the famous excavations in Winchester between 1962-75, masterminded by Martin Biddle, served as a model for, amongst others, Henri Galinié's recent investigations in Tours[13], France. British urban archaeology has also served as a model for the rapid

---

13 For Winchester, see for example Martin Biddle (ed.), *Winchester in the Early Middle Ages (Winchester Studies 1)*, (Oxford 1976), For Tours: Henri Galinié, Tours, in R. Hodges & B. Hobley (eds.), *The rebirth of towns in the West, AD 700-1050*, (London 1988), 57-62.

development of field archaeology in Italy. Excavations in Brescia, Milan, Rome and Verona, for example, during recent years explicitly used techniques pioneered by the Department of Urban Archaeology at the London Museum[14].

It might be claimed, therefore, that Medieval Archaeology has come of age. But has it? In fact, the discipline still faces a serious problem. Clearly, it is no longer an antiquarian subject, the results of which are deployed only to fill museum cases and to illustrate the margins of history books. Without any doubt, over the past twenty-five years a scientific data base has been created, much as historians of the Middle Ages established in the 19th century when they ensured the transcription and publication of the major written sources (principally the *Monumenta Germaniae Historica*). Yet, just as historians in the earlier half of this century began to appreciate that it is not sufficient to amass information, so Medieval Archaeology is at the point of trying to make some sense of what it is doing. In short, it is seeking to become a historical social science[15].

Few archaeologists and historians have followed the works of Arbman and Jankuhn with analytical studies of Medieval

---

14 See Francovich, *op. cit;* for examples see Daniele Manacorda & Enrico Zanini, The first millennium A.D. in Rome: from the Portus Minucia to the via delle Botteghe Oscure, and G-P. Brogiolo, Building transformations in a Lombard city, in K. Randsborg (ed.) *The Birth of Europe. Archaeology and social development in the First Millennium A.D.* (Analecta Romana Instituti Danici Supplementum XVI) (Rome 1990), respectively 25-32 & 156-65; also C. La Rocca Hudson, "Dark Ages" a Verona. Edilizia privata, aree aperte e strutture pubbliche in una città dell italia settentrionale, *Archeologia Medievale* XIII (1986), 31-78.

15 Similar discussions are also taking place amongst Byzantinists: Marcus L. Rautman, Archaeology and Byzantine Studies, *Byzantinische Forschungen*, XV (1990), 137-65.

Archaeology which challenge the documentary historian's perspective of this period[16]. Picture books about the Vikings, or studies of the Migration Period treating the data as explicit ethnic traits giving flesh to the ethnohistorical skeleton are still commonplace. Steps to change this, though, have been taken. Departments of Medieval Archaeology have been set up in universities throughout Western Europe. These exist now in the universities of Aix-en-Provence, Arhus, Caen, London, Lund, Siena and Wurzburg, while lectureships in Medieval Archaeology can be found in about a quarter of the university archaeology departments in Europe. This, however, is still a very fragile foothold when one considers the huge volume of field archaeology devoted to the medieval period. Bearing in mind all the excavations and their analysis afterwards, Medieval Archaeology probably accounts for over fifty per cent of all archaeological activity in Western Europe. Furthermore, the prospects for greater co-operation with historians, as well as with managers of Europe's cultural heritage has never been better. Archaeologists are now interested in the changing configurations of life in the Middle Ages. Modern social and economic historians are finding a reservoir of new data, while, the Jorvik Centre at York, for example, recreating the archaeology of the 10th. century Viking town, has proved an exceptional attraction to almost a million visitors every year.

Let me illustrate the dawn of this new phase in the history of Medieval Archaeology with a few examples.

---

16 An obvious exception is Klavs Randsborg, whose books *The Viking Age in Denmark*, (London 1980) and *First Millennium A.D. in Europe and the Mediterranean*, (Cambridge 1991) have proved to be influential. Note also the work of Heiko Steuer: for example: Archaeology and History: Proposals on the Social Structure of the Merovingian Empire, in K. Randsborg (ed.), *The Birth of Europe. Archaeology and Social Development in the First Millennium A.D.* (Analecta Romana Instituti Danici Supplementum XVI), (Rome 1990), 100-22.

II

THE END OF ANTIQUITY

The whole concept of the Dark Ages has grown out of fascination with classical culture. Put rather simply, the barbarian invasions and migrations were used by the contemporary authors of the first millenium to account for the end of antiquity. The barbarians provided an explanation for an otherwise seemingly inexplicable problem – the breakdown of "civilization". This thesis, albeit in much more sophisticated form, is still maintained by many archaeologists and historians although it overlooks two fundamental issues. First, classical antiquity was clearly suffering from tremendous economic and social problems long before the so-called invasions and migrations[17]. Secondly, unlike classical antiquity which undoubtedly collapsed in most every respect (see below), the Middle Ages, despite intermittent crises not unlike those encountered in antiquity, survived and gave rise to modern Europe. Paradoxically, modern Europe is the ultimate expression of roots planted during the fall of the Roman Empire, yet it is the Empire rather that its founding fathers which has captured its attention.

This interface between antiquity and the Middle Ages has attracted historians for over a century. Karl Marx and Friedrich Engels[18], for example, exchanged many letters

---

17 Randsborg, *First Millennium* (note 16) for a synthesis of a great deal of debate about the so-called third-century crisis and its aftermath.

18 See E. Hobsbawn's edition of Karl Marx, *Pre-capatalist economic formations,* (London 1964).

debating the problems of this period. But, taking into account the poverty of the written sources, it has only been in last two decades that we have any real measure of the transformations enacted during this critical period. In Italy, the heart of the Empire, the gradual decline of many towns after the 3rd century is now an incontestable fact. North of the Alps, the complete abandonment of Romano-British towns in the later 4th century is now documented not only in London and York, but in most smaller centres[19]. At the same time, the gradual decay of Roman villas, not only in Britain but also in Gaul and Italy, can be charted with some precision as a result of fine stratigraphic excavation techniques. Finally, as classical antiquity was first and foremost an agrarian peasant society, the archaeology of tenant farmers is most telling. Field surveys, ranging from those carried out around Rome or the Appennines to those in the English Pennines, reveal the inexorable decline in the number of sites over the 3rd and 4th centuries, and the staggering transformation of the rural community[20].

But this was not a holocaust – a moment of catastrophic change. Quite the reverse, the configurations of the western world were changing slowly, generation by generation. Now, through careful excavations and field surveys the archaeologist can chart the demise of many towns, villas and farms and the survival of some in a modified, often shambling form. At the same time new centres and communities sprung up.

---

19 Martin Millett, *The Romanization of Britain: an essay in archaeological interpretation,* (Cambridge 1990); Randsborg, *op. cit.*

20 See Graeme Barker & John Lloyd (eds.), *Roman Landscapes Archaeological survey in the Mediterranean region,* (London 1991) for reviews of recent surveys; see Randsborg, *First Millennium,* for general analysis; see Richard Hodges, *Wall-to-Wall History. The Story of Roystone Grange,* (London 1991) for a Pennine illustration of rural developments in later Roman times.

For example, the 4th century witnessed the supplanting of Rome by Constantinople as the pre-eminent Mediterranean town. This was bound to alter the rhythms of trade, commerce and regional life in the Western Empire. It was also certain to affect the social and economic circumstances in provinces like Gaul and Britain, as well as the conditions of those territories beyond the Roman frontiers with economics linked to it. Hence, for awhile, at least, the archaeology of 4th century Denmark shows that this region flourished. A new port of this age has recently been discovered at Lundeborg in south-east Funen close to a major ritual centre at Gudme[21]. Finds of Roman goods as well as evidence of crafts show that Lundeborg was a major centre, taking advantage of a boom in Baltic Sea economic activity at exactly the moment that North Sea trade, hitherto controlled by the Romans, was slumping in recession.

It is into this context that we have to fit the invasions and migrations. But we need to be scientific and ask: what are the sources for these invasions and migrations? Who described them, and why? Why do we ascribe the distinctive burial artefacts to these peoples? What new light does our finer understanding of the rhythms of regional settlement patterns throw upon these artefacts? The Anglo-Saxons, for example, are largely unknown from 8th century and later texts. These texts were written for a purpose: to give some written legitimacy to kings seeking to demonstrate their claims to be the heirs of a long and distinguished tradition. Without any doubt, there is a kernel of truth in these texts. However, the challenge facing the historian is to disentangle the facts from the propoganda, an ideological device often

---

21 P. O. Thomsen, Lundebord 1. Havn og handelsplads fra 3. og 4. århundrede efter Kr., *Årbog for Svendborg & Omegns Museum*, 12-52; Klavs Randsborg, Beyond the Roman Empire: archaeological discoveries in Gudme on Funen, Denmark, *Oxford Journal of Archaeology* 9 1990, 355-66.

invented long after the events described in the sources. It is a wholly false step to assume that a new burial pattern and thus all the articles contained in the graves can be directly equated with the arrival of a new people[22]. In the Anglo-Saxon case, for instance, eighty per cent of the Anglo-Saxon graves belong to a period some hundred years or so after the invasions described in the written sources. Meanwhile, the so-called Anglo-Saxon were inhabiting peasant dwellings of a form which were common in Britain during the Roman period. In short, with new means of measuring the life-style of these peoples we can begin to appreciate that this was a critical period in the history of England, but that generations of archaeologists and historians have misinterpreted the sources. What transpired, as in cases where we have good anthropological descriptions of the eclipse of one culture by another, was far more complex, and indeed intriguing.

---

22 Heiko Steuer, *op. cit.*, (note 16); Richard Hodges, *The Anglo-Saxon Achievement*, (London 1989), 10-42.

III

THE DARK AGES

Modern excavations show beyond any doubt that the Dark Ages represent an important stage separating antiquity from the High Middle Ages. For many years the nature of this separation has fuelled a compelling debate amongst archaeologists. Some argue that there was a good deal of continuity between the Roman and medieval worlds, while others favour discontinuity. The question of continuity has been fostered, of course, because the medieval written sources tend to emphasise the link with the Roman age. This is hardly surprising as latin was the pre-eminent language used in written texts throughout the millennium, and words signifying town, a country-house etc. were not likely to be changed, even if these took entirely different forms, for example, in the 1st and 9th centuries. On the other hand, the archaeological evidence tends to emphasise discontinuity. The archaeological record is made up of strata which invariably highlight moments of great activity. Moments of low activity, by contrast, tend to be poorly represented. It is easy, therefore, to use the written sources to suggest a picture of slowly, unfolding change, and the archaeological sources to show a picture of sudden dramatic change, followed by inactivity. Great importance is bound to be attached to finding ways of connecting the two sources. Dendrochronlogy, because it enables us to obtain such an accurate date for the felling of a piece of timber, now offers perhaps the best opportunity to obtain a truly historical date for archaeological activity and inactivity.

The question of continuity has been most fiercely contested

about towns in the post-Roman period. In 20th century Europe, a highly-urbanised society in which rural production is managed by less than 10% of the population, it is difficult to imagine a world without market towns. Yet, excavations in countless West European towns show that urban life was virtually extinguished between the 4th and 7th centuries, and only revived during the 10th century[23]. Many archaeologists have been truly surprised to discover this, having imagined that an 8th century reference to a market-place means that evidence of a more-or-less unaltered version of a Roman town, and the predecessor of the better-documented 10th century town might be found. The reality is very different. Much of Rome, Florence, Milan, Cologne, Paris, Utrecht, Canterbury, London and Winchester – to name a few places – contain nothing more that "black earth" in this period. This thick layer of fine, humic loam has mystified many people, but long before samples of it were analysed by geomorphologists, it could be explained by visiting any derelict part of a modern city. In fact, it is a compound of vegetation and wind-blown particles that accrues very quickly in Western Europe[24]. It is the product of desertion and urban degeneration.

Town life, of course, was not wholly forgotten in Western Europe. No-one seriously doubts that Rome, for example, was entirely abandoned. Despite serious depopulation, the ancient city continued to be used by many small monastic communities who occupied islands within the dereliction. The same was probably the case in many traditional Roman

---

23 See the range of essays on this theme in R. Hodges & B. Hobley (eds.) *The rebirth of the town in the West, A.D. 700-1050,* (London 1988).

24 For a scientific study of black earth see R. Macphail, Soil and botanical studies of the Dark Earth, in M. Jones & G. W. Dimbleby (eds.), *The Environment and Man,* (Oxford 1981), 309-31.

centres. Cologne, for example, was the seat of an archbishopric with a cathedral community that occupied a small part of the once great Romano-Gallic city. Winchester, similarly, was occupied by several small communities, perhaps concerned with the minister. Of course, these were not towns in the medieval sense of the term. But then were there towns in the sense that we interpret the word in antiquity? The distinguished ancient historian Sir Moses Finley has argued convincingly that the ancient city was a centre for consumption – for an elite – rather than a place primarily concerned with craft production and commercial activities. In a telling phrase he writes: 'it seems commonly overlooked that the excavators of Tarsus have found no Cloth Hall, that all ancient cities lacked the Guildhalls and Bourses which, next to cathedrals, are to this day the architectural glories of the great medieval cities of Italy, France, Flanders, the Hansa towns, or England. Contrast the Athenian Agora with the Grande Place in Brussels'[25]. Finley's concept of the ancient city is a place for consumption.

So where will we find the roots of the medieval town? Archaeology is beginning to suggest it has a genesis in three rather different origins. The first may be the Mediterranean town in late antiquity, when public amenities were appropriated by craftsmen and traders. Commonly, the forum area was colonised by makeshift workshops. For example, this occurred at Gloucester and Silchester in Britain, and in any number of towns around the Mediterranean during the 5th-7th centuries[26]. It is not entirely clear how this

---

25 M. I. Finley, The Ancient City: From Fustel de Coulanges to Max Weber and beyond, in M. I. Finley, *Economy and Society in Ancient Greece*, (Harmondsworth 1983), 3-23, at 18.

26 For Britain see Millett, *op. cit.* (note 19); for a general review of the town in late antiquity see Randsborg, *First Millennium.*

transformation occured, although it may reflect an attempt by the urban secular and ecclesiastical elite to control craft production close to the seat of their power.

The second and most obvious origin of the medieval town was, amazingly, almost unknown to historians unitl recently. This is the trading emporium. The written sources described places like Dorestad, Hamwic, Hedeby, and Quentovic, but nothing really prepares us for what this places looked like in reality. In AD 700, when the Venerable Bede was an adolescent, most settlements in the Merovingian kingdom or in Anglo-Saxon England covered no more than 1-2 hectares in area. Palaces and monasteries, even the celebrated community at Jarrow in Northumbria, contained a matter of dozens of people. By contrast, Dorestad covered more than 40 hectares, and had a population of thousands; Hamwic, Anglo-Saxon Southampton, covered some 45 hectares and had at least 4000 inhabitants; and the newly discovered port of Quentovic, south of Calais, well-known from the sources, certainly was as large as these other two emporia, if not larger[27].

A striking feature of these towns is that they began as trading stations, and then became steadily concerned with the kind of regional production and commerce that, as Finley pointed out, is the hallmark of the medieval town. Contemporary writers appear to have been careful not to describe these places, so it has become the archaeologist's job, as Arbman and Jankuhn first recognized more than fifty years ago, to bring them to the attention of historians. A notable feature of Hamwic, where the topographical evidence survives best

---

27 Richard Hodges, *Dark Age Economics,* (London 1982); *idem,* Charlemagne's elephant and the beginnings of commoditisation in Europe, *Acta Archaeologica* 59 (1988), 155-68; David Hill et al, Quentovic defined, *Antiquity,* 64 (1990), 51-58.

of all, is that it was planned as though it was a Roman town with a street grid that includes a broad central street. King Ine of Wessex was almost certainly the architect of this ambitious undertaking, but did he imitate a derelict Roman town in Wessex like Winchester or did a monk that had been on a pilgrimage describe to him what towns in Italy looked like[28]?

The 8th-century geography of the emporia also confounds traditional historical thinking. Hamwic and the newly-discovered emporia at Quentovic, London, Ipswich and Eoforwic (York) all belonged to a trade network linking the Neustrians and the Anglo-Saxon kingdoms. At the same time there existed a parallel network of ports, comprising Dorestad and Domburg in the Low Countries to Medemblik in Frisia and Ribe in western Jutland[29]. At this time, though, as far as we can tell, there were no comparable ports around the western Mediterranean. Indeed, nothing resembling Hamwic has been so far discovered in Italy. By the age of Charlemagne, it is possible that small trading centres may have been established in the Veneto at Aquilea or Venice, possibly at Rome, and in the ports of Gaeta, Naples and Salerno in the Kingdom of Beneventum, but the evidence remains very slight as yet.

Around the North Sea, though, the significance of these places can be gauged by the foundation of Hedeby with a street-grid, dated accurately by dendrochronology – a

---

28 Hodges, *The Anglo-Saxon Achievement,* 80-92.

29 Hodges, *Dark Age Economics,* 47-86; J. Besteman, The pre-urban development of Medemblik, in H. A. Heidinga & H. H. van Regteren Altena (eds.), *Medemblik and Monnichendam. Aspects of Medieval urbanization in northern Holland,* (Amsterdam 1990), 1-30; Mogens Bencard & Lise Bender Jorgensen, The foundation of Ribe, *Antiquity,* 64 (1990), 576-83.

planned town – almost certainly designed to replace the 8th-century western Jutish port of Ribe (near Esbjerg). Hedeby illustrates most persuasively that the pagan, illiterate Danes were not the savages the sources depict, but a tribal society that in many ways was closer to the economic mainstream of Latin Christendom than much of Italy[30].

The third root of the medieval town lies in the activities of the Church. The Church provided the intellectual and scientific connection with antiquity, safeguarding a knowledge that was often anachronistic to the small, under-populated communities of the Dark Ages. Yet here, we may suspect, was a reservoir of skills that proved vital as the need to create towns became more compelling. Archaeology once again has revealed the modest size of this reservoir, and is beginning to show how it might have become a major feature of the Carolingian age (see below).

What is beyond dispute now – because countless excavations in countless towns provide a rich archaeological documentation – is that the medieval town, as we know it, is a feature of the 10th and 11th centuries. Drawing upon these three very different roots, an urban revolution encompassed Western Europe from Norway to Sicily, from Ireland to Russia. It did not happen simultaneously everywhere. Wessex and Northumbria, for example, had full-scale market towns long before northern France. Denmark had market towns two hundred years before Early Christian Ireland. But by AD 1100 the enduring concept of a regional hierarchy of communitites, concerned with industrial production and marketing, had taken shape.

---

30 Hodges, Charlemagne's elephant and the beginnings of commoditisation in Europe (see n. 27); Bencard & Bender Jorgensen, *op. cit.*, (note 29).

IV

MOHAMMED AND CHARLEMAGNE

The true maturing of medieval history as a discipline came with the posthumous publication of Henri Pirenne's brilliant, if controversial book *Mohammed and Charlemagne* (1937). Pirenne argued that the migrant tribes of the 4th to 6th centuries preserved what political institutions they could and did not deliberately destroy classical civilization. In his opinion it was the Islamic conquest of North Africa and the eastern Mediterranean during the 7th and early 8th centuries which led to the overthrow of Roman mastery of the Mediterranean. This was the nexus of change, leading to the collapse of urban life in the West, and the concentration of power in a landed aristocracy. It was the Emperor Charlemagne who, by allying himself with the Papacy, reversed this situation. The sources indicate that his government promoted commerce in the North Sea and, simultaneously, the rejuvenation of the old Roman Empire. In a most famous passage, Pirenne concludes: 'It is therefore strictly correct to say that without Mohammed Charlemagne would have been inconceivable. In the seventh century the ancient Roman Empire had actually become an Empire of the East; the Empire of Charles was an Empire of the West...The Carolingian Empire, or rather, the Empire of Charlemagne, was the scaffolding of the Middle Ages'[31].

Such a contentious book aroused a powerful debate. Pirenne's interpretation of the 7th century was soon shown to be weak,

---

31 Henri Pirenne, *Mohammed and Charlemagne*, (London 1937), 234-5.

especially as excavations of Byzantine ports in western Anatolia revealed an economic crisis long before the rise of Islam. Yet, in the absence of archaeological data the circumstances surrounding the age of Charlemagne appeared somewhat confusing. On the one hand, as German historians pointed out, Charlemagne ruled the greatest expanse of territory in Europe between the end of the Roman Empire and the rise of Napoleon. On the other hand, although Charlemagne ruled rather longer than Napoleon, the two reigns are similar insofar as they appear to be little more than bellicose interludes in European history. Recent archaeological research offers a valuable insight into this age, to some extent confirming the essential tenet of Pirenne's thesis.

There are three striking features of the archaeology. The first of these is the development of commercial links beyond the Carolingian Empire. The heartland of the Empire appears to have fostered two trading networks. Frankish traders from Neustria seemed to be occupied with markets in England (at Hamwic etc.), while Rhenish products, such as swords, quernstones, sweet wine, tablewares, glasses were handled by Frisian merchants, many of whom were based in Dorestad. This trade was destined for Frisia and Denmark. Denmark, of course, lay outside the bounds of the Empire, so the construction of the planned town of Hedeby in c.810 as a terminus for this trade reflects its importance (see above). but what could the Carolingians gain from this commerce with the Danes? The archaeology of Hedeby offers an answer. Here was the western end of a network of a complex web of Scandinavian trade-routes, connected to other trading operations down through western Russia, and ultimately linked to the Abbasid Caliphate with its court at the new, round city of Baghdad. As excavations at Viking ports like Birka and Hedeby testify, this was the circuitous route by which precious metals, include large quantities of silver, as well as silks, spices and other oriental ornaments reached northern and western Europe. For about thirty years between 790-820 this was one way that two very different cultures, Christendom and Islam, might exchange goods. To avoid the heretical action of direct exchange, pagan traders including Frisians and Vikings acted as the middlemen. Of course, the Carolingian world did come into direct contact with the Abbasids. Three embassies were exchanged, and on one occasion an elephant was despatched to Charlemagne as a gift. It seems, too, that the Beneventans, like the Danes located just beyond the borders of the Empire, dealt directly with the Aghlabids of the Maghreb. Pope Leo III, however, once roundly condemned the Beneventans, though there is little doubt that the fruits of this trade, notably gold, were sent to Charlemagne from time to time as tribute[32].

This commerce is important for two reasons. First, though it only lasted for a short period, it served to emphasise the widespread relations between the different parts of Europe for the first time in several centuries. Second, it provided Charlemagne with gifts to buy support from the aristocracy in his farflung territories; it also provided a reservoir of silver

---

32 Hodges, Charlemagne's elephant (see n. 27); see also A. O. Citarella and H. M. Willard, *The Ninth-Century Treasure of Montecassino,* (Montecassino 1983). For a review of the Duchy, later Kingdom of Benevento, especially under Arichis II, when Benevento and Salerno were effectively revived as urban centres, see Paolo Peduto, Insediamenti longobardi del Ducato di Benevento (secc. VI-VIII), in Stefano Gasparri & Paolo Cammarosano (eds.), *Langobardia,* (Udine 1990), 307-80. A probable illustration of a consignment of tribute sent from the Duchy of Benevento to the Carolingians was found in 1857 in the river Reno, near Bologna. It comprised over a hundred gold coins, of which 39 were examined, and found to be 23 Byzantine solidi, 5 Beneventan solidi and 11 abbasid dinars: see Giovanni Gorni, Moneta e scambi nel Veneto altomedievale, in Andrea Castagnetti & Gian Maria Varanini (eds.), *Il Veneto nel Medioevo. Dalla "Venetia" alla marca Veronese,* (Verona 1989), 187-88.

which could be used for coinage and devising a monetary economy.

The second feature revealed by the archaeology is far more intriguing. During this period it seems that many monasteries were granted privileges and encouraged to assume a new identity. The concept of the monastic retreat was replaced by that of the centre promoting christianity. Excavations of Benedictine monasteries like those on the island of Reichenau in southern Germany, at Müstair in Switzerland, and San Vincenzo al Volturno in Molise (what was Beneventum) were transformed from tiny communities focussed around a simple church into huge bodies of monks and lay-servants managing what were by the standards of the times, small towns[33]. Obviously the most striking feature of this age was the strident use of classical themes as part of a renaissance. Excavations throughout Latin Christendom reveal a momentous change in the scale of church-building in this era, as the small, primitive structures of the 8th century were replaced by ambitious churches that prefigure the cathedrals of the high middle ages. The excavations at San Vincenzo al Volturno emphasise that paintings and the use of writing were prominent features of all parts of the monastery. Furthermore, the distinguished guests' palace here belongs to the widespread revival of the Roman triclinium, and can be paralleled to examples now known all over Latin

---

33 The literature on the archaeology of early medieval monateries is growing fast. The essential text is Walter Horn and Ernest Born *The Plan of St. Gall,* (Berkeley 1979), which for all its faults is a truly exceptional study. Of the many critiques of Horn & Born, perhaps the most illuminating is Adalbert de Vogne, Le Plan de Saint-Gall, copie d'un document officiel? Une lecture de la lettre a Gozbert, *Revue Benedictine* 94 (1984), 295-314. For a general overview of the problem, as illustrated by the archaeological discoveries made at one monastery, see Richard Hodges, *A Dark Age Pompeii: San Vincenzo al Volturno,* (London 1992).

Christendom at this time, including one recently excavated at Northampton in Mercia, and another splendidly preserved at Naranco in the old christian kingdom of Asturias (in northern Spain). In sum, the architecture and art of the elite during a brief period followed a pattern that Charlemagne himself set in the construction of his palaces at Aachen and Ingelheim. beyond all doubt. The ideological unity described in the texts of this era was given material expression by an investment in construction and artistic expression.

The third feature of the archaeology of this age in many ways made the architecture and art possible. In a nutshell this was the promotion and exchange of scientific knowledge. Remains of concrete-mixers have been found in most parts of the Empire, illustrating how techniques of making cement were re-introduced to parts where in the interval clay-based mortars had been in use. This facilitated the making of large basilican buildings in place of the small chapels of the Merovingian age. Similarly, techniques of glass-making were widely desseminated to produce the material to light these buildings. Indeed, the extensive excavations at San Vincenzo al Volturno suggest that construction-workers, architects, painters, glaziers, glass-workers, tile-makers, potters, and smiths were all brought and accommodated in the monastery as to manage the transformation from a retreat to a centre of civilization. For a generation, only, the monastery was like a small town, from which skills were probably diffused to the monastery's estates[34]. But there are signs that production techniques were not just being overhauled in the monasteries. In the Rhineland during this period many small potters' workshops were deserted in favour of craft villages in the Vorgebirge

---

34 Hodges, *Dark Age Pompeii* (n. 33); for an illustration of the archaeology of pre-10th-century towns in which the dual forces of the monastery and the king are present see Galinié, *op. cit.*, (note 13).

Hills, west of Bonn. Here traditional potting techniques were improved, and new vessel forms as well as new decorative techniques were introduced. Gradually some of these ideas were diffused to potters not only in France, but in England as well[35]. Similarly, metallurgical analyses of metals from this age show that old labour-intensive techniques of making iron were replaced by the revival of carbonising the implements. At the same moment an excavation of an iron foundry in Wessex shows that Roman slag-tapping techniques were reintroduced to improve the overall efficiency of the metallurgical process[36].

Besides the changes to these crafts, it is evident that new ideas about field management, in particular rotation of fallow, was introduced during this period to estates in Hesse. Field surveys in England, notably at Wharram Percy, suggest that the same innovations were adopted by the Anglo-Saxons at this time, creating the well-known configurations of medieval field systems. Studies of animal husbandry from the Low Countries and parts of England suggest a greater emphasis on managing stock-breeding, with programmed cycles of

---

35 Richard Hodges, *The Hamwih Pottery: the local and imported wares from 30 years' excavations at Middle Saxon Southampton and their European context,* (London 1981), esp. 86-89.

36 Jeremy Haslam, A Middle Saxon iron smelting site at Ramsbury, Wiltshire, *Medieval Archaeology* 24, (1980), 1-68; Richard Hodges, The beginnings of the medieval iron industry in western Europe: craft specialisation and the domestic mode of production, in *Medieval iron-making and the role of the oldest process industry in medieval society,* (Stockholm 1985), 299-307.

culling. At the same time there are signs that improved strains of cereals were being introduced[37].

But it is far from clear that these innovations swept across the length and breadth of the Carolingian world. It seems more probable that there were islands of great activity, separated by densely wooded and thinly populated landscapes. What the archaeology makes clear is that many of these developments were short-lived, and perhaps dependent upon the political charisma of Charlemagne himself. The trading networks, for example, began to decline as early as the 820's, long before the advent of the Vikings as a menacing threat. The cultural renaissance also ground to a halt in the second quarter of the 9th century. But the revival of scientific concepts ranging from agrarian practice to making cement or iron was not lost. Such ideas were to be Charlemagne's real legacy to the Middle Ages – a scaffolding in more senses that Pirenne perhaps appreciated.

---

37 See, for example, H.-J. Nitz, Settlement structures and settlement systems of the Frankish central state in Carolingian and Ottonian times, in Della Hooke (ed.), *Anglo-Saxon Settlements*, (Oxford 1988), 249-73; Hodges, *The Anglo-Saxon Achievement*, 136-42. W. Prummel, *Early Medieval Dorestad: an archaeozoological study. Excavations at Dorestad 2*, (Amersfoort 1983).

V

THE VIKINGS

The Vikings enter history as perpetrators of catastrophe. some historians have seen them as the last barbaric episode of the migration period. Most regard them as catalysts of change. In fact, the Vikings are essentially the preserve of prehistorians. Apart from runic texts, they left little other than archaeology as a legacy of their age. Western history, however, has adopted a perspective of them taken from the Anglo-Saxon and Frankish written sources which runs counter to the archaeology. Why is this?

The first point to consider is that contrary to modern thinking about the concept of a Dark Age, the 8th and 9th centuries, to judge from the available archaeological data, were essentially peaceful. Telling illustrations of this are the absence of fortifications around Dorestad, Hamwic or Quentovic, and of private or institutional fortifications generally. The great dykes of this age, Offa's dyke separating Mercia and Wales, and the Danevirke separating Denmark from the Carolingian kingdom were almost certainly conceived as political boundaries. The advent of medieval fortification can be pinpointed quite accurately to the central and later decades of the 9th century when the open emporia at London and York appear to have been deserted in favour of the old walled Roman settlements nearby. It was at this time, too, that Pope Leo IV built the defences around the Vatican and encouraged the construction of the new hilltop site a Centocelle (Lazio) in place of his vulnerable port at

Civitavecchia[38]. From this period also date the Carolingian fortified hilltop palaces in Hesse and the aristocratic ringworks, such as Hunneschans in the Rhine delta of Holland[39].

The second point to take into account is that the Danes were caricatured as savages by missionaries like St. Willibrord in the early 8th century, nevertheless it is plainly Victorian piety to believe that religious zeal was the only reason for the mission in the first place. Willibrord will have found an urban community at Ribe, not unlike Hamwic, where silver deniers (the so-called Wodan Monster sceattas) were minted in large numbers. If he travelled across Jutland he might have seen the extraordinary canal cut through the island of Samsø. Likewise, some eighty years later in 808, Charlemagne's anger with King Godfred of the Danes was almost certainly aroused by the impudent foundation of Hedeby, and the threat it posed to his control of Baltic Sea trade with the Carolingian Empire. The construction of Hedeby as a planned town, resembling in some respects a small Roman city, should not leave us in any doubts about the capability of the Vikings. Excavations of villages like Vorbasse in Jutland show that this was a highly stratified tribal society. These were not savages. Furthermore, the recent discovery of the remains of a 9th-century water-mill at Omgård in Jutland demonstrates that the Frankish concept of milling was established in Denmark some three hundred years before any

---

38 Sheila Gibson & Bryan Ward Perkins, The surviving remains of the Leonine wall, *Papers of the British School at Rome*, part I, 47 (1979), 30-57; part II, 511 (1983), 222-39 .. On the fortified town of Centocelle see: Odoardo Toti, *La Cittá Medioevale di Centocelle (854-1462)*, (Civitavecchia 1988).

39 H. A. Heidinga, The Hunneschans at Uddel reconsidered: some ideas about the function of a medieval ringfort on the Central Netherlands, (*Chateau Gaillard* XIII 1987), 53-62.

written source describes it[40]. As in its urban life, it appears that the Viking community was emulating the most advanced economic developments in the Carolingian world.

Such developments were probably not diffused uniformly to all parts of the Scandinavian world, any more than they were to the Carolingian Empire. Nevertheless, field surveys of Gotland and excavations in the Mälar valley of central Sweden show, just as Stolpe pointed out in the 19th century, that these were at the hub of farflung trade networks. The cemetery at Birka, for example, boasted the remains of traders from all who originated from all parts of the Baltic. The imaginative and dynamic art of the Vikings, like the Carolingian Renaissance, skillfully captures the mood of this age[41].

It is not difficult, therefore, to see why the Anglo-Saxons and Franks caricatured the Vikings in the way they did. They were pagans who were imitating the major trends of Latin Christendom. Once Christendom entered a recession in the 820's and 830's, largely triggered by internal political dispute, it was very easy to look beyond to the Vikings to find an explanation for their plight[42]. Moreover the recession itself within the Carolingian Empire must have created economic hardship in the Baltic world. For a while at least trade and raiding seem to have become almost indistinguishable, as

---

40 Hodges, Charlemagne's elephant (see n. 27); Randsborg, *The Viking Age in Denmark* (note 16); also, Bencard & Bender Jorgenson, *op. cit.*, (note 29).

41 This, in essence, was the rationale for Holger Arbman's pioneering study: *Schweden und das karolingische Reich*, (Stockholm 1937), described above.

42 On the recession see Richard Hodges & David Whitehouse, *Mohammed, Charlemagne and the Origins of Europe*, (London 1983), 158-68; see also Randsborg, *First Millennium;* also, Michael Metcalf and Peter Northover, Coinage alloys from the time of Offa and Charlemagne to c.864, *Numismatic Chronicle*, 149, 1989, 101-20.

when Viking traders in AD 845 raided the merchant's quarters outside the bishop's palace at Hamburg, a short sea-journey from Denmark. Unlike the Carolingian Empire, though, the powerful social and economic momentum of the early 9th century in Denmark did not disappear.

Interestingly, Charlemagne's biogragher, Einhard, looking back to the formative years of his master's reign, commented 'if a Frank is your friend, he is not your neighbour'. Now, it was the turn of the Vikings to inherit the mantle of the Franks in West European history. A generation of raiding, especially in England, Scotland, Ireland and northern France, has distracted attention from the fact that in the last decades of the 9th-century Danish and Norwegian kings were building towns like Jorvik, Lincoln and Dublin and developing land management schemes which were worthy of the Carolingians two generations before. In short, in many ways they were not so much the last barbarians, as among the first to successfully wear the medieval mantle devised by Charlemagne[43].

Like the Arab raiders menacing Italy and southern France at this time, the Vikings have been the victims of vulgar history. Modern archaeology causes us to reappraise the ideology of the texts we possess. It shows that the Scandinavians had a heritage which had withstood the collapse of antiquity, and had evolved unaffected by the Latin Church. As each piece of their archaeology is discovered we are learning to ask new questions about these peoples. This in turn compells us to re-examine our views about the christian sources that until now have dominated our views about the christian, monkish sources that until now have been the principle source for the main thrust of European history.

---

43 Hodges, *The Anglo-Saxon Achievement,* 157-62.

VI

INCASTELLAMENTO

The Italian concept of *incastellamento* has been described extensively by historians, who have made full use of the extensive survival of land charters from the 10th century[44]. But the term usefully serves to illustrate another area of European medieval history being brought to light by recent archaeology. the process of developing towns, like the process of nucleated villages, seems to form part of a general phenomenon. The written sources register this process for the first time not only in terms of the aristocracy and clerical elite, who made history, but also the peasantry who invariably are ignored by those who made the texts.

The paramount mark of this age is the revival of town life throughout all parts of western Europe. Craft production that had been restricted to the emporia or monasteries was now practised in centres of different sizes in every region[45]. Successive generations then created the conditions for the integration of town and country life. In some regions, such as Beneventum, the Rhineland and Wessex, this evolved swiftly; in others, such as eastern Denmark, northern France,

---

44 For an exemplary introduction to *incastellamento* in Italy see Chris Wickham, *Early Medieval Italy,* (London 1981), 163-7 as well as his *The Mountains and the City,* (Oxford 1988); note also Guy Bois, *La Mutation de l'an mil.* (Paris 1989). A recent summary of archaeological work on *incastellamento* in Italy can be found in *Archaeologia Medievale* XVI 1989, 15-288.

45 Hodges, *Dark Age Economics,* 162-84.

Provence and Tuscany, this appears to have evolved more slowly. The pattern of this evolution and the reasons for it are, of course, matters that archaeologists need to examine in far more detail in the future. A second feature of this age is the huge productivity. The three 10th-century tenements excavated at Coppergate in York produced evidence of 2-3 tons of pottery discarded as rubbish in their backyards! The same volume of material is conspicuous at 11th-century Norwich, Schleswig, Tours or Xanten. Discarded commodities on a similar scale are also apparent at villages such as Raunds in Northampton or Montarrenti in Tuscany. A third feature of this age is the prominent place of the manor and church n the rural and urban landscapes. Stone-built castles become a regular occurence in Anglo-Saxon and Frankish villages from the middle of the 10th century. Parish churches were also constructed in large numbers at this time in all parts of Christendom. Up to some 5,000, it has been estimated, were built in the second half of the 10th century in England alone. But in all parts of western Europe, unlike the great abbey churches, these tended to be simple buildings that initially, at least, were barely decorated[46]. Each of these features formed a critical part in the fabric of western Europe on the eve of the new millennium. Each enables the archaeologist to examine the regional pathway to feudalism, as the world of late antiquity was finally eclipsed.

Strangely, it is with the inception of feudalism that the archaeological record becomes weaker. As the written sources increase in number. and pose more intriguing questions, so there is a need for more archaeological research. The prospects are good as the sites awaiting analysis are plentiful. Here, however, the collaboration between the archaeologist

---

46 Richard Morris, *Churches in the Landscape,* (London 1989), 165-67; Hodges, *The Anglo-Saxon Achivement,* 180.

and historian has to be close, as at stake is an understanding of why the medieval tradition has endured. This, perhaps, as the medieval world reassumed the global dimensions of the Roman one, is an area for future archaeological research that promises to reveal as much about the second millennium, as it has done for the first.

FURTHER READING

The bibliographic notes are principally to works in English, though readers are urged to make use of journals such as *Acta Archaeologica, Archeologie Medievale, Archeologia Medievale, Berichten van de Rijksdienst voor het Oudheidkundig Bodemonderzoek* (the journal of the Dutch State archaeological service), *Frühmittelalterlichen Studien, Journal of Danish Archaeology, Papers of the British School at Rome, Zeitschrift für Archaologie des Mittelalters.*

J. Besteman, J. M. Bos & H. A. Heidinga (eds.) *Medieval Archaeology in the Netherlands,* (Assen 1990).

Roger Collins, *Early Medieval Spain,* (London 1983).

Wendy Davies, *Wales in the Early Middle Ages,* (Leicester 1982).

Richard Hodges, *Dark Age Economics,* (London 1982).

Richard Hodges, *The Anglo-Saxon Achievement,* (London 1989).

Richard Hodges & David Whitehouse, *Mohammed, Charlemagne & the Origins of Europe,* (London 1983).

Richard Hodges & Brian Hobley (eds.), *The Rebirth of Towns in the West A.D. 700-1050,* (CBA Research Report No. 68), (London 1988).

Walter Horn & Ernest Born, *The Plan of St. Gall,* 3 vols., (Berkeley 1979).

Edward James, *The Origins of France,* (London 1982).

Richard Krautheimer, *Rome: a Profile of the City 312-1308,* (Princeton 1980).

Bryce Lyon (ed.), *Carlomagno e Maometto: Bisanzio, Islam e Occidente nell' Alto Medioevo,* (Milan 1986).

Cyril Mango, *Byzantium,* (London 1980).

P. Perin & L-C Feffer, *La Neustrie* (Rouen Museums), (Rouen 1985).

Klavs Randsborg, *The Viking Age in Denmark,* (London 1980).

Klavs Randsborg, *The First Millennium A.D. in Europe and the Mediterranean,* (Cambridge 1991).
Klavs Randsborg, *The Birth of Europe. Archaeology and Social development in the First Millennium A.D.*, Analecta Romana Instituti Danici Supplementum XVI, (Rome 1990).
Chris Wickham, *Early Medieval Italy,* (London 1981).
David Wilson (ed.), *The archaeology of Anglo-Saxon England,* (London 1976).

ARCHAEOLOGICAL JOURNALS

Acta Archaeologica:
Acta Archaeologica,
c/o Institute of Archeology,
Vandkunsten 5,
DK-1467 Copenhagen K,
Denmark

Published by:
Munksgaard,
35 Nørre Søgade,
PO Box 2148,
DK-1016 Copenhagen K,
Denmark

Archeologia Medievale:
Archeologia Medievale,
Facoltá di Lettere,
Universitá degli Studi di Siena,
Via Roma 56,
53100 Siena,
Italy

Published by:
Archeologia Medievale,
(Edizioni) All' Insegna del Giglio
S.A.S.,
Via R. Guiliani 152r,
50141 Firenze,
Italy

Archéologie Médiévale:
Archéologie Médiévale,
Publications du centre de
recherches archéologiques
médiévales,
Université de Caen,
F-14032 Caen Cedex,
France

Published by:
Éditions du Centre National
de la Recherche Scientifique,
15, Quai Anatole,
Paris,
France

Berichten van Riiksdienst voor het Ouheidkundi Bodemonderzoek (R.O.B.):
R.O.B.,
Rijksdienst voor het Ouheidkundig Bodermonderzoek,
Kerkstraat 1,
3811 CV Amersfoort,
Netherlands

Frühmittelalterliche Studien:
Dr Mechthild Sandmann,
Institut für
Frühmittelalterforschung
der Univerität Münster,
Salzstraße 41,
D-4400 Münster,
Germany

Published by:
Walter de Gruyter & Co.,
D-1000 Berlin 30,
Germany

Journal of Danish Archaeology:
Journal of Danish Archaeology,
Odense University Press,
36, Pjentedamsgade,
DK-5000 Odense C,
Denmark

Papers of the British School at Rome:
British School at Rome:
Regent's College,
Regent's Park,
London NW1 4NS,
Great Britain

Zeitschrift für Archäologie des Mittelalters:
Zeitschrift für Archäologie des Mittelalters,
Rheinland Verlag GmgH,
Köln,
Germany